INSIDE THE BLUES

12-Bar Blues
The Complete Guide for BASS

by
Dave Rubin

PAGE		TRACK
2	Dedication	
3	Introduction	
	Tuning	1
6	Blues Bass Scales	
7	Country Blues	2–6
12	Chicago Blues	7–16
22	Texas Blues	17–26
32	Swing Blues	27–31
37	Rhythm & Blues	32–36
42	Jazz Blues	37–41
47	Blues-Rock	42–46
52	Funk Blues	47–51

PLAYBACK+
Speed • Pitch • Balance • Loop

To access audio visit:
www.halleonard.com/mylibrary
Enter Code
1862-2416-0037-5517

T0057819

ISBN 978-1-61780-867-8

Visit Hal Leonard Online at
www.halleonard.com

Contact Us:
Hal Leonard
7777 West Bluemound Road
Milwaukee, WI 53213
Email: info@halleonard.com

In Europe contact:
Hal Leonard Europe Limited
42 Wigmore Street
Marylebone, London, W1U 2RN
Email: info@halleonardeurope.com

In Australia contact:
Hal Leonard Australia Pty. Ltd.
4 Lentara Court
Cheltenham, Victoria, 3192 Australia
Email: info@halleonard.com.au

DEDICATION AND ACKNOWLDGMENTS

I would like to dedicate this book to the legendary "Groovemaster," bassist Jerry Jemmott. Thanks to Edward Komara and Eric LeBlanc for their invaluable assistance with researching the history of blues bass. In addition, the notes to Dick Spottswood's *How Low Can You Go?* (Dust-to-Digital, 2006) provided a great source for the early history of the string bass.

INTRODUCTION

Acoustic Roots

It's hard to imagine that there was a time when people believed the bass should be "felt, more than heard" and, even more condescendingly, that "you do not really notice the bass but would miss it if it was not there." Of course, there is a grain of truth in both statements, most obviously the latter—though anyone who does not "feel" the pounding low end emanating from subwoofers in heavy metal and rap, for example, needs to check their pulse! In the blues, however, the bass has become the "pulse" that propels a slow blues forward like the relentless torque of a vintage John Deere tractor, or drives a charging shuffle like a team of country mules. On top of that, the bass also provides a roadmap of the harmonic changes and, in power-trio blues, literally supplies an outline of the chords during solos that don't have a rhythm guitar or keyboard laying down the harmony.

The double bass, contrabass, bass viol, string bass, bass fiddle, upright acoustic, "bull fiddle," or "doghouse bass" eventually became the bottom end in blues and jazz as the intertwined original American art forms developed in the years following the Civil War. The legendary, mythical, and unrecorded New Orleans cornetist Buddy Bolden led a band during the 1890s and early years of the 20th century that reportedly played both genres, and a famous photo of his band exists from 1905 showing string bassist Jimmy Johnson, in addition to guitarist Jefferson "Brock" Mumford. As opposed to most North American string bands of the era that utilized the tuba for the lower frequencies, "N'Awlins" string groups often contained double basses under guitars, mandolins, and violins for indoor gigs—as opposed to brass instrumentation outdoors. However, it took until the mid-1920s and thereafter for the string bass to begin to supplant the tuba and other brass instruments on recordings due to both the technical shortcomings of the acoustic-horn recording process and the prevailing straight-up 4/4 stride rhythms. Recording equipment could not capture the nuances and lower frequencies of brass instruments, and rhythmic foundations evolved into more more malleable and demanding swing and shuffle rhythms—unlocking the potential of the four-string thumper. Swing placed more responsibility on the technical skills of everyone, and it became apparent that a plucked bass was a far more practical instrument for maintaining the accelerated tempos of the new jazz. Nonetheless, in 1930 the top dance-band leaders like Fletcher Henderson, Louis Armstrong, and King Oliver were still relying on the tuba for the bottom register (though Duke Ellington was an exception). However, by 1932, both the tuba and the banjo had been effectively replaced by the bass and guitar, respectively.

The first blues string bassist of note was William Manuel "Bill" Johnson (1872-1972). In a long and productive career, Johnson played with various blues pioneers, including Tampa Red. Bassist Walter Sylvester "Hoss" Page (1900-57) contributed mightily to the growing popularity of the instrument and, as an innovator of "walking bass," to the development of 4/4 swing (initially with his Original Blue Devils, and later with Count Basie). Bandleader and arranger Fletcher Henderson, one of the architects of swing music, sometimes employed bassist Ralph Escudero, who occasionally backed early blues "divas" such as Trixie Smith, Bessie Smith, and Ethel Waters. The classic female blues singers of the 1920s rarely used string bassists, though Bessie Smith, the "Empress of the Blues," occasionally employed Cyrus St. Clair. At her last session, in 1933, bassist Billy Taylor, from Buck Washington's band, provided the "bottom line."

Country and Delta blues guitarists in the 1920s and 1930s mainly played solo, rarely working with second guitarists or harmonica blowers. However, in 1930, acoustic country blues guitarist Carl Martin and bassist Roland Armstrong began recording as the Tennessee Chocolate Drops, with Martin on bass and Armstrong on guitar. In 1935, they waxed an excellent duet, "Good Morning, Judge," and a string of blues recordings in Chicago that utilized the bass. These included "The Dozen" (cut two days after "Good Morning, Judge"), featuring Big Bill Broonzy (vocal and guitar), Jazz Gillum (harmonica), and, most likely, William Lee "Bill" Settles (1917-80) on the upright. Like Bill Johnson, Settles, who is credited with the introduction of "slap bass," likewise had a lengthy and distinguished career, backing up a wide array of artists such as Ma Rainey,

Washboard Sam, Lil Johnson, Blind Blake, Casey Bill Weldon, Bumble Bee Slim, and Dinah Washington. In Chicago, prewar blues would be spearheaded by Broonzy, with Settles, Wilbur Ware, Oliver Hudson, and Ransom Knowling plucking the big bull fiddle on his behalf. Broonzy's friend and fellow Chicago blues king Tampa Red (Hudson Whittaker) and his Hokum Boys also played with Settles, while Memphis Minnie (Lizzie Douglas), the last (but not least) of the trio of Chicago blues guitar masters, presumably employed him, as well, on her recordings with her beau, Charlie McCoy, in the 1930s.

By the time T-Bone Walker began his recording career in earnest in 1940, the string bass was firmly established in the urban blues dance bands of the era such as those of Les Hite and Freddie Slack. His recordings in New York, Los Angeles, and Chicago through the WWII years and beyond contain a variety of bassists, including William King "Billy" Hadnott (1914-99)—who went on to accompany everyone from Charlie Parker and Louis Jordan to Lloyd Glenn and B.B. King. During the late 1940s, Johnny Moore (with and without Charles Brown) employed Eddie Williams and Johnny Miller, respectively, on the big upright.

In 1948, Muddy Waters made history by officially ushering in electric Chicago blues when he recorded "Can't Be Satisfied" b/w "Feel Like Going Home" with bass man Ernest "Big" Crawford providing essential harmony and percussion with his "slapped" patterns. Echoing the tradition of country blues bass that traced back to Bill Settles, his lines "skipped" rather than "walked." He appeared on Waters' early classics through approximately 1954, when William James "Willie" Dixon arrived. As arguably the most influential Chicago blues bassist and songwriter, Dixon (1915-92) had been performing with vocal groups since 1939, before connecting with Chess Records, where he also became a producer and talent scout. His mature style encompassed both country and walking bass lines and can be heard on his work with Chuck Berry (Chess Records) and other Cobra Records artists.

Electric Bass

The desire to amplify the acoustic guitar and bass had been kicking around at least since the twenties, when Lloyd Loar, the creator of the famous archtop L-5 for Gibson (1924), experimented with an electric double bass. (Gibson also made a rather inefficient acoustic, fretted "Mando Bass" from 1912 to the thirties.) The acoustic resonator guitars of Dobro and National were louder than flattop and archtop guitars but still limited, and amplifying the bass was even more of a challenge. Popular history credits Rickenbacker, Les Paul, and Leo Fender with significant innovations, while acknowledging Fender as the producer of the first successful solidbody electric bass. However, his 1951 Precision bass, shaped like the Telecaster, is often misidentified as the *first* to be manufactured, when, in fact, Paul H. Tutmarc (1896-1972) actually achieved that goal in 1933. Tutmarc's first instrument resembled a cello, which he eventually considered too large. But this experiment would lead him to produce the 1936 "Model 736 Bass Fiddle" (and companion guitar) at his Audiovox Mfg. Co. in Seattle, Washington, which vaguely resembled a rounded off sixties SG or Vox Phantom. Though roughly 100 basses were mass produced, Tutmarc was an inefficient promoter, and neither innovation caught on.

In the thirties, both Rickenbacker and Regal weathered unsuccessful attempts to amplify upright basses. In the late forties, bassist Everett Hull began making amplified doublebasses by putting a microphone inside via the peg on the bottom of the instrument. This "amplified peg" became "Ampeg" and the renowned company was born, but this bass—like virtually all previous attempts—proved unpopular. Consequently, until the fifties, electric blues guitarists would sometimes detune their instruments and play bass lines on the lower strings in lieu of an upright bassist. Though clearly not the first, Fender's remarkable "P-Bass," with its punchy, booming, aggressive sound and easy playability, completely revolutionized the role of the bass player to the extent that, for many years, the musicians union listed it as a separate category.

Monk Montgomery (1921-82), brother of jazz guitar giant Wes Montgomery, is generally acknowledged as the first electric jazz bassist. In the blues, it appears to be Thurber "Sam-Guy" Jay who played electric with Louis Jordan on a May 28, 1953 session for Decca Records, some six months before bandleader Lloyd

Lambert (1928-95) first backed Guitar Slim on Slim's Specialty recordings, in October of 1953. Lambert also played on Slim's Atco/Atlantic sides through 1958, as well as with Little Richard and Ray Charles, and is recognized as one of the first to play the Fender Precision bass, in addition to an early Gibson solidbody electric bass. By the late fifties, Willie D. Warren (with Otis Rush) and Dave Myers (with the Aces) were leading the charge on the electric bass in Chicago for all who followed.

In the intervening years, many bassists have made their presence known, including Ransom Knowling, who made the transition to electric with Robert Nighthawk; Mack Thompson (Magic Sam); Jack Myers (Buddy Guy, Junior Wells); Willie Kent (Little Walter, Eddie Taylor, bandleader); Donald "Duck" Dunn (Booker T & the MGs, Albert King, others); Larry Taylor (Canned Heat, others); Jerry Jemmott (Aretha Franklin, B.B. King, many others); Johnny B. Gayden (Albert Collins); Tommy Shannon (Johnny Winter, Stevie Ray Vaughan); Richard Cousins (Robert Cray); Randy McDonald (Tommy Castro); and Michael Merritt (Shemekia Copeland, others).

Despite advances in digital technology (along with sampling and synthesizers), there is still no substitute for the picked, plucked, slapped, or snapped long-scale string of a bass in the blues. Though occupying the nether regions of the sonic spectrum, the bass is the heartbeat of the music.

BLUES BASS SCALES

Shown below are the scales that we'll use throughout this book, all in the key of G. Notice that each scale has been written out three times, relative to the I (G), IV (C), and V (D) chords in the key of G. We'll start with common root-position fingerings for the Ionian mode (or "major" scale) and those blues bass scales derived from it: the minor pentatonic scale, Mixolydian mode, composite blues scale, Aeolian mode (or "minor" scale), and Dorian mode.

Ionian (Major) Mode – Key of G

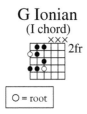

G Ionian
(I chord)

C Ionian
(IV chord)

D Ionian
(V chord)

O = root

Minor Pentatonic – Key of G

G Minor Pentatonic
(I chord)

C Minor Pentatonic
(IV chord)

D Minor Pentatonic
(V chord)

Mixolydian Mode – Key of G

G Mixolydian
(I chord)

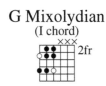

C Mixolydian
(IV chord)

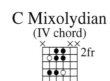

D Mixolydian
(V chord)

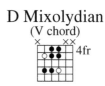

Composite Blues Scale – Key of G

G Composite Blues
(I chord)

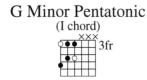

C Composite Blues
(IV chord)

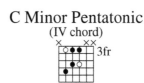

D Composite Blues
(V chord)

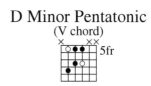

Aeolian (Minor) Mode – Key of G

G Aeolian
(I chord)

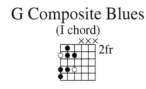

C Aeolian
(IV chord)

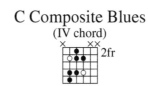

D Aeolian
(V chord)

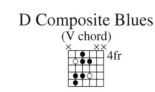

Dorian Mode – Key of G

G Dorian
(I chord)

C Dorian
(IV chord)

D Dorian
(V chord)

COUNTRY BLUES

For purposes of illustration and expediency, this book uses the term "country blues" to describe virtually all blues, including the urban variety of Leroy Carr and that found in Chicago in the early and mid-thirties, before the commercial electrification of guitars in 1938.

Country Blues No. 1

The utilization of root/5th notes for each chord change is one of the oldest accompaniment strategies in 20th-century American music. Heard in prewar blues, jazz, popular, and country music, it especially lives on in traditional country songs. Here (in the key of E major), it involves the root (E) and 5th (B) of the I chord, the root (A) and 5th (E) of the IV chord, and the root (B) and 5th (F#) of the V chord. Examples may be heard in the early recordings of Muddy Waters (1948-49), with Big Crawford slapping the "doghouse" bass.

Performance Tip: Use your ring finger to access the root and 5th of each change so as to place your frethand in an advantageous position for the chromatic runs.

Country Blues No. 2

The Mixolydian mode relative to the I, IV, and V chords is the bedrock blues bass scale. It first appeared on record in the era of the Classic Women Blues Singers of the twenties, when the tuba or the left hand of the pianist often provided bass lines. An effective bass player always connects the I and IV chords smoothly and logically, as shown in measures 1 and 2. But remember to vary your runs, since the same walking Mixolydian lines for all three changes can become predictable. Note the addition of the ♭3rd (B♭) from the G blues scale (following the B natural) in measure 8. Likewise, see the hip chromatic line in measure 10—the root (C), ♭2nd (C♯/D♭), and 2nd (D). The 3rd (E) that concludes measure 10 (and also appears in measure 6), almost functions as a motif preceding the G change in measures 7 and 11.

> **Performance Tip:** Play the first note in measures 1 and 2 with your middle finger; the first note in measures 3, 4, 7, 8, and 9 concludes with your ring finger; and the first note in measures 4, 6, 10, 11, and 12 with your index finger.

Country Blues No. 3

This classic descending line is found in the early Chicago blues of Muddy Waters and others, and leans heavily on the ♭7th (D and G) and ♭6th (C and F) of the I (E) and IV (A) chords, respectively, creating a gritty sound that hearkens back to Delta blues. The ♭6th is not in the Mixolydian mode but it adds an ominous feel and completes the chromatic cadence to encourage forward motion. The ♭6th also leads smoothly and chromatically to a satisfying resolution on the 5th (B) of E in measure 12, during the turnaround. Also note the steady eighth-note rhythm, which is a prime characteristic of walking bass patterns.

> **Performance Tip:** Play the chromatic sequences with your ring, middle, and index fingers, respectively.

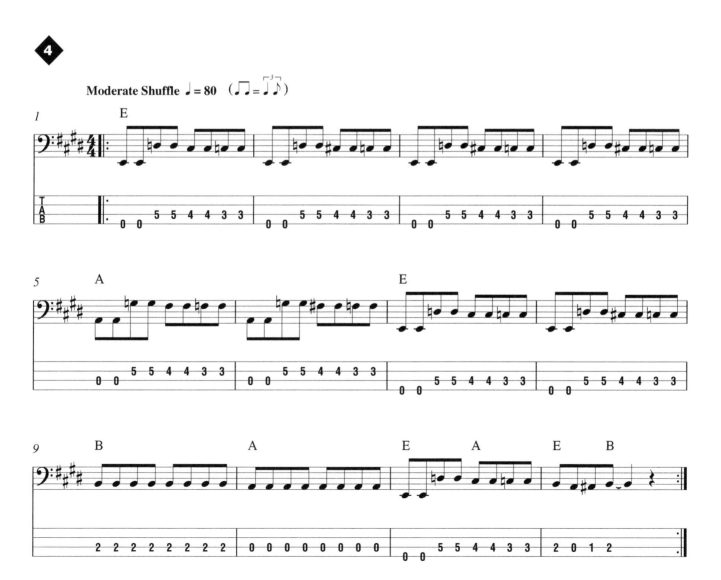

Country Blues No. 4

Boogie woogie has contributed mightily to walking blues bass lines. It first showed up on the guitar in the South (as early as the 1880s), and then was developed to high art on the piano by Pete Johnson, Meade Lux Lewis, and Albert Ammons, circa WWII. The piano variety tended to feature the root, 3rd, 5th, and 6th notes, from either the Ionian or Mixolydian modes, for an upbeat, "happy" sound. Check out the steady flow of quarter notes that descend and ascend in graceful arcs, especially the powerful forward momentum in measures 11 and 12, the turnaround. Here, instead of resolving to and ending on the V (D) chord, the bass line remains on the I (G) chord for a dramatic, two-octave ascending line.

Performance Tip: All descending lines begin with the pinky or middle finger, and all ascending lines begin with the middle finger.

Country Blues No. 5

The immortal Bessie Smith and her "classic" peers enjoyed the backing of Dixieland jazz cats who began bringing sophisticated ideas to the table in the pre-swing, pre-walking bass line era of the twenties. Right off, notice the move from the 5th (D) to the ♭5th (D♭) in measure 1, which injects tart blues tension, before quickly resolving to the tonic (G). Alternating between tension and resolution is the hallmark of the blues and can also be seen in measure 3, where the spicy ♭3rd (B♭) is emphasized, while the root (G) and ♭7th (F) notes appear in measure 4 to complement the tonality of the chord change. Do not miss the unusual V (D) to ♯V (D♯) chord change in measures 9 and 10, respectively—a sure sign that standard 12-bar changes had not yet been codified.

Performance Tip: In measure 9, use your index finger as a moving bar across the strings to access the D major tones.

CHICAGO BLUES

Chicago Blues No. 1

In the fifties, the walking bass lines of Howlin' Wolf, Muddy Waters, and other Chicago blues acts started to show evidence of the "modern" blues bass to come, as they began swinging eighth notes and playing longer, two-measure ascending and descending lines. They also began injecting chromaticism into measures 7–8 of the blues form, which you'll find in the following example. The concept is particularly effective in measures 11 and 12 (during the turnaround), where the chromatic line directly connects the I (A) chord to the V (E) chord. Check out how measures 9 and 10 contrast with the rest of the form. Here, over the V (E) and IV (D) chords, walking lines are substituted with simple tonic and 5th notes.

Performance Tip: Alternate between your right-hand index and middle fingers as much as possible as you pluck the strings, especially for eighth-note pairs or long "strings" of eighth notes.

Chicago Blues No. 2

In the forties, there was popular interest in Cuban and Latin American music, which danced its way into the blues of T-Bone Walker, among others. In Chicago and other blues hotspots, Cuban and Latin American music was being included in new compositions by the fifties, adding previously unrealized rhythmic vitality to songs like B.B. King's "Woke Up this Morning" (1953). Sometimes found in minor key progressions, these lines were derived from the rumba and other sun-drenched tropical dances. Though seemingly repetitive at first glance, note the subtle variations—such as in measure 4, where the tonic (E) repeats, instead of the 5th (B), so as to add implied 5th–root movement to the IV (A) chord in measure 5.

Performance Tip: You can use your index finger throughout, if you find that approach easiest.

Chicago Blues No. 3

A swinging shuffle featuring exclusive quarter notes and walking Mixolydian lines provides for an upbeat sound that is occasionally found in the more "commercial" compositions of Willie Dixon, like "Jump Sister Bessie" (1957) by Otis Rush. This line is sweetened considerably by the root (B♭)–6th (G) move in measures 1, 3, and 7 (the I chord). Note the change of direction in measure 4 (I chord) from an expected descending line to an ascending line that moves through the 3rd (D), 4th (E♭), and 5th (F)—fluidly connecting to the root (E♭) of the IV chord in measure 5.

Performance Tip: Alternate your right-hand index and middle fingers, striving for equal volume and a strict meter that swings.

Chicago Blues No. 4

Here's a faster jazzy shuffle that goes beyond strict walking Mixolydian lines and incorporates dynamic direction changes into the lines. Observe how the G♯ (string 2, fret 6) functions as both the 6th of the I (B) chord and the major 3rd of the IV (E) chord. In addition, notice the "imperfect cadence" in measures 9–10, where the V chord (F♯) connects to the IV chord (E) via a chromatic line—3rd (A♯) to ♭3rd (A) to 2nd (G♯). Note that the G♯ functions as a 2nd over the F♯ chord; it also functions as the implied major 3rd of the upcoming E chord. Likewise, the 6th (C♯) on beat 4 of measure 10 makes for a strong one-step move to the tonic (B) in measure 11.

Performance Tip: In measure 9, use your pinky and index fingers exclusively.

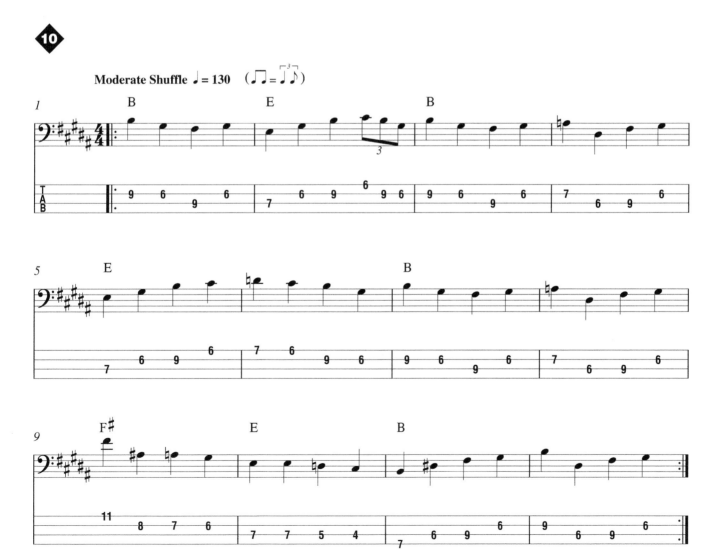

Chicago Blues No. 5

Here's a pattern that is similar to the verse of "All Your Love (I Miss Loving)" (1958) by Otis Rush. The eighth-note line that ascends chromatically from the 5th, through the ♭7th and major 7th, provides powerful resolution to the tonic note in every measure.

Performance Tip: Play each tonic and 5th with your ring finger, and then walk up from the ♭7th with your index, middle and ring fingers, respectively.

Chicago Blues No. 6

This line features a variety of rhythms in each measure that build momentum—from half notes to swung eighth notes to triplets—to create a surging, syncopated pattern that would contrast dynamically with basic 7th and 9th guitar comp chords. A rhythmic "Spanish tinge" (as coined by Jellyroll Morton) could be employed by the other instruments in an ensemble for a feel similar to the Albert King version of "Crosscut Saw" (1967). Check out the II–V (instead of V–IV) chord change in measures 9 and 10, which is outlined with a classic ascending and descending line that employs the D composite blues scale (i.e., blues scale plus Mixolydian mode) and the G Mixolydian mode, respectively. Additionally, hear how the root, 5th, and 6th notes that begin each I and IV chord produce a "happy" sound.

Performance Tip: Start every measure, except numbers 9 and 10, with your middle finger.

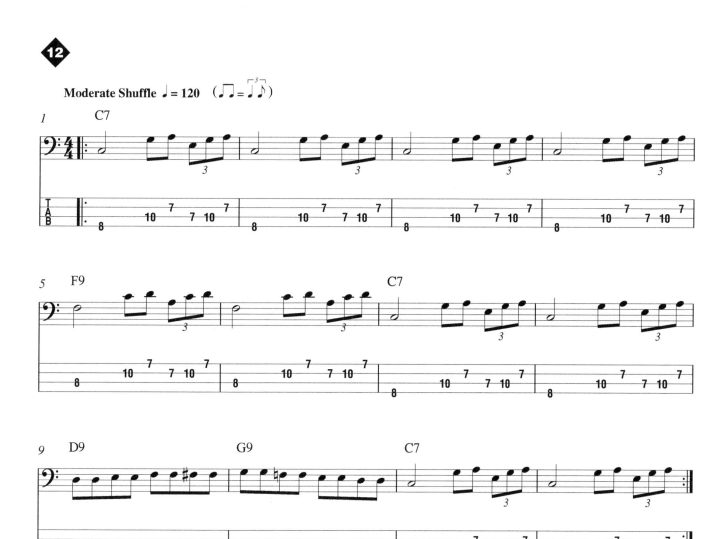

Chicago Blues No. 7

The dramatic octave jump seen in this pattern (measures 1–11) is a basic tenet of Chicago blues, and was frequently heard in Buddy Guy's classic sixties Chess tracks, such as "I Got My Eyes on You" (1960). (It also appeared in the fifties, on the early Chess recordings of Lowell Fulson.) The descending chromatic line in each measure (save for the turnaround, in measure 12) combines the major 7th from the Ionian mode with the ♭7th from the Mixolydian mode for an effect that is both melodic and bluesy. The triplets in measure 12 contribute a welcome and dynamic change of pace from the steady stream of swung eighth notes.

Performance Tip: Utilize a sequence of your index, pinky, ring, middle, index, pinky, and index fingers to play measures 1–11.

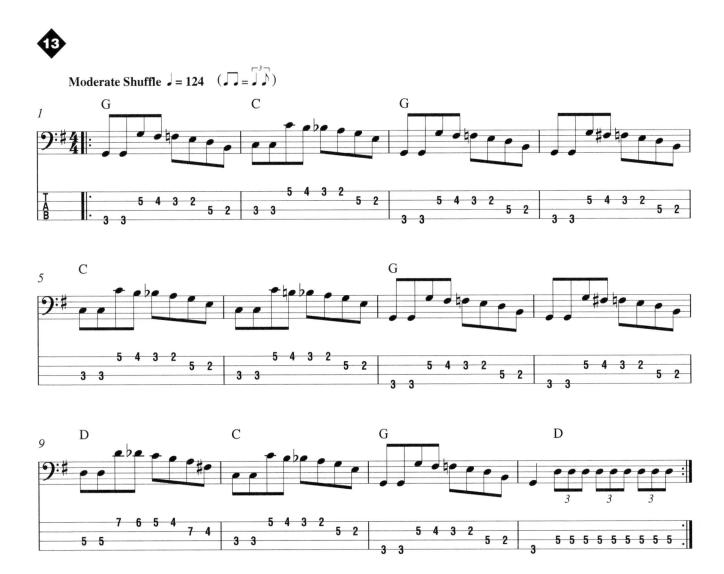

Chicago Blues No. 8

The minor pentatonic scale relative to each chord change makes a dandy and obvious choice for a minor-key blues. Be aware that the iv (Fm) chord also can be accessed at fret 8, starting on string 3; the v (Gm) chord can be accessed two frets higher, at fret 10. However, keeping the pattern on the fourth string and dropping the register to the first fret engenders a more consistent sound, as well as a darker, more dramatic effect that is appropriate in minor keys.

Performance Tip: Though it is a stretch in the lower positions, try to use the index and pinky fingers to move from the second note to the third note of each chord change.

Chicago Blues No. 9

It is always advisable to vary blues bass lines unless they function as a motif or hook, or are played in unison with another instrument. This is especially important in slow blues tunes, wherein more implied space naturally occurs. Notice the *six* different rhythmic patterns here among the I, IV, and V changes (the pattern in measure 1 appears only *once*). Also notice how the momentum increases in each measure (similar to "Chicago Blues No. 6"), a characteristic of blues phrasing that often occurs in lead instrumental solos. As befits the turnaround, extra forward motion, via sets of triplets, helps move to the next 12-bar verse. Check out how the E composite blues scale (i.e., blues scale plus Mixolydian mode) is arranged to imply I–IV–I–V movement in this turnaround.

Performance Tip: Use your ring finger for the 3rd (G♯) at fret 4 of the fourth string in measures 1, 3–4, 7–8 and 11–12. This sets your hand up to efficiently play the rest of the notes in each measure.

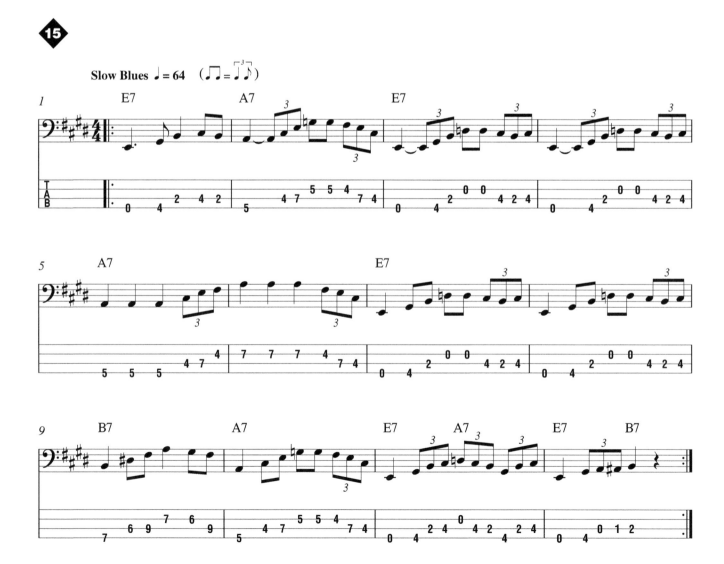

Chicago Blues No. 10

A hint of the modern blues to come in the sixties and beyond is revealed by the churning triplets on beats 2–4 of each measure. As previously shown in "Chicago Blues Nos. 5, 6, and 9," measures that contain increasing divisions of the beat provide additional momentum and drive, even in a slow blues. A certain amount of drama, often inherent in slow blues, is also created by the sustained root note in every measure, except the final two. Pay attention to how the ♭7th (E♭, A♭, and B♭ for the I, IV, and V chords, respectively), as the first note in each triplet (on beats 3 and 4), accentuates the dominant quality of the Mixolydian bass lines.

Performance Tip: Over the I (F7) and IV (B♭7) chords, use your index and ring fingers for the first and third notes of each triplet, respectively.

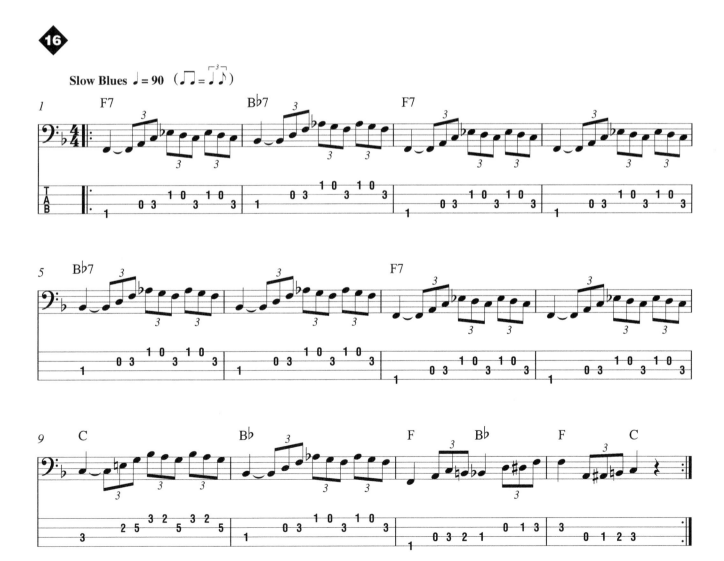

TEXAS BLUES

Texas Blues No. 1

The distinction between Chicago blues and Texas blues is not always clear, or other regional designations for that matter, as their roots in country blues tend to be similar. The octave jump is regarded as a Chicago blues characteristic, but Texan Ray Sharpe utilized it on his hit "Linda Lu" (1959). Be sure to notice how the bass line, which could have been a very repetitive, one-measure pattern throughout, is varied with a "walk-up" from I to IV (E to A) and from I to V (E to B) in measures 4 and 8, respectively, and with the descending line in measures 5 and 6. Furthermore, measure 9 (V chord) changes the rhythm and direction of the bass line, while measure 10 (IV chord) walks deliberately from the root (A) to the root of the I chord (E) in measure 11. Finally, notice the hip turnaround, which involves propulsive chromatic lines.

Performance Tip: In measures 10–11, assign your index, middle, ring, and pinky fingers to frets 4–7, respectively.

Moderate Shuffle ♩ = 120

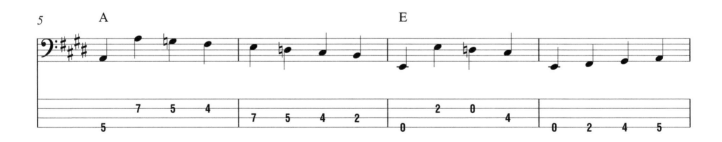

Texas Blues No. 2

Fast walking bass lines comprised of swinging quarter notes may be traced back to Walter Page, since Southwestern "territory bands" that he toured with (like that of the legendary Count Basie) greatly influenced the "swing" of Texas blues. Observe how all of the lines in this example are in two-measure increments, including measures 9–10 (over the II and V chords), where a classic pattern seen previously in "Chicago Blues No. 6" appears. Check out the line in measure 4 (over the I chord, E), which walks *down* from the root (E) to the 5th (B), and then continues down a whole step to the root of the IV chord (A) in measure 5 for an accelerating effect.

Performance Tip: Play the descending line in measures 2 and 4 with the following sequence: pinky, middle, index, and pinky.

Texas Blues No. 3

The "jass" (original archaic spelling) starts to make its presence felt in the slow minor key blues, with Dorian mode lines for the i (Cm) and iv (Fm) chord changes in measures 1–8. The descending patterns add to the implied somber quality of minor key progressions, while the ascending line on beat 4 of measures 6 and 10 (over the iv chord) provides variety and forward momentum back to the I chord. Check out measure 9, where a simplified rhythm dynamically and dramatically slows the action, and a chromatic sequence walks down to the root of the iv chord (F), in measure 10. Also note the well-oiled turnaround (measures 11–12), which walks between all three chords.

Performance Tip: Begin measures 1–11 with your ring finger, but use your index finger to start measure 12.

Texas Blues No. 4

Creating variety within walking blues bass lines can be challenging because virtually all of them are phrased in a quarter-note swing rhythm. One way you can add variety is by reducing the "color palette" (note choice) to basic major triads (root, 3rd, and 5th). Observe the "jazzy" use of the 2nd (or 9th, D) in conjunction with the ♭7th (B♭) over the IV chord (C9) in measures 2 and 10. Likewise, the 2nd is emphasized on beats 3 and 4 of measure 6 (IV chord), where it provides anticipation to the root of the I chord (G) in measure 7. Yet another useful variation is found in measure 3 (I chord), where the 4th (C) appears between the two 3rds (B) for a jolt of musical tension. The 4th similarly appears in measure 8 (I chord) as tension that is resolved handsomely to the 5th (D) and root (G) that follow. Conversely, pay attention to how that C note functions as the root of the IV chord in measure 11, while the D conveys the 5th of the I chord in measure 12.

> **Performance Tip:** In measures 1, 4, and 9, employ your ring finger for both the D note and the G note at fret 5.

Texas Blues No. 5

This brisk blues shuffle, comprised of strict swung quarter notes, encroaches even further on the jazzman's turf. It contains waves of ascending and descending lines, almost all of which connect by half or whole steps for one long, seemingly unbroken, rush of notes—similar to the way Tommy Shannon often supported Stevie Ray Vaughan. Check out how the composite blues scale (i.e., blues scale plus Mixolydian mode) relative to each chord is skillfully mined for forward motion and hipness. This approach is especially noticeable in measures 9 and 10 (over the V chord, B7), where the root (B) is mostly tucked away while notes like the ♯5th (G/F✗) create tremendous anticipation for the upcoming resolution to the root of the I chord (E)—which mercifully occurs in measure 11.

Performance Tip: In measures 4, 7, and 11, lead off with your middle finger, and in measures 5 and 6, start with your pinky.

Texas Blues No. 6

Maximum momentum is achieved in another fast shuffle via smooth-as-polished-leather lines that either connect chromatically or by walking Mixolydian mode patterns. One exception occurs, for variety, in measure 9 (over the V chord, F#). To avoid needless repetition, only measures 1, 2, and 3 repeat (in measures 11, 12, and 7, respectively). The unbroken thread from measure 4 to measure 8 is a marvel of logical note selection, as the I (B), IV (E), and I chord changes are navigated with the appropriate composite blues scale (i.e., blues scale plus Mixolydian mode). Do not miss the cool line in measures 1 and 11, which dynamically moves *down* in pitch from the root (B) to the 3rd (D#) and then ascends to the 4th (E) and ♭5th (F).

Performance Tip: Start measures 1, 2, 3, 4, 6, 7, 8, 11, and 12 with your pinky.

Texas Blues No. 7

As befits jazz-bred Texas blues, the Aeolian mode, or "natural minor," is the more melodic and sophisticated minor key scale of choice (instead of minor pentatonic, more commonly used in other locales). Though the Aeolian mode relative to the i (Gm), iv (Cm), and v (Dm) chords is applied appropriately, do not miss the major 3rd (B natural) on beat 4 of measure 1, which boosts the change from the i chord to the root of the iv chord (C), in measure 2. Likewise, notice how the last note in almost every other measure leads strongly to the succeeding measure either by 5th–root movement (D–G in measures 2–3; G–C in measures 4–5) or step-wise ♭7th–root movement (C–D in measures 8–9). The eighth-note phrasing in measures 1, 4, 5, and 6 contributes to the propulsion and always occurs following straight quarter notes.

Performance Tip: As opposed to most major key blues, the Aeolian lines in each measure may be started with your index finger.

Texas Blues No. 8

This upbeat shuffle is reminiscent of the boogie blues that Gatemouth Brown pioneered in the late forties and early fifties and was assimilated by the next generation of Texas blues cats. The prominence of the 6th degree of the Mixolydian mode (or the Ionian mode, in this case) also is similar to the Western Swing music of the thirties and forties that flourished in the Lone Star State and throughout the southwest. Observe that each measure basically consists of the root, 5th, and 6th notes, though measures 1–3, 7, and 11 also contain the major 7th (C♯) "leading tone" on the "and" of beat 4. Note how measure 4 contains the 3rd (F♯) on the "and" of beat 4, which functions as the major 7th "leading tone" of the IV chord (G), in measure 5.

Performance Tip: Begin measures 1–5, 7–8, and 11–12 with your middle finger. Use your pinky to start measures 6, 9, and 10. Use your index finger for the last note of measures 1–4, 7, and 11.

Moderate Shuffle ♩ = 132

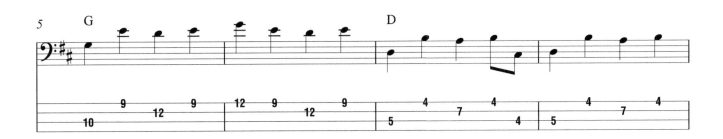

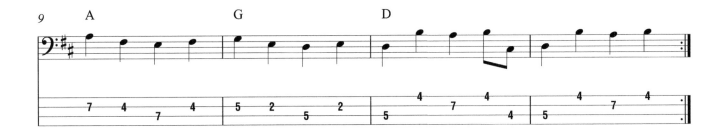

Texas Blues No. 9

A classic Texas bass line that is heard in the blues of Lowell Fulson and Freddie King, to name just two luminaries. The octave-jumping Mixolydian-mode lines for the I (C7) and IV (F7) chords frolic around the beat with the grace of an antelope leaping across the plains. Measures 9 and 10 substitute the II–V (D7–G7) chord change for the typical V–IV (G7–F7) change, while the classic ascending and descending line previously seen in "Chicago Blues No. 6" and "Texas Blues No. 2" makes another guest appearance.

Performance Tip: Assign one finger per fret, with your index finger handling the seventh fret.

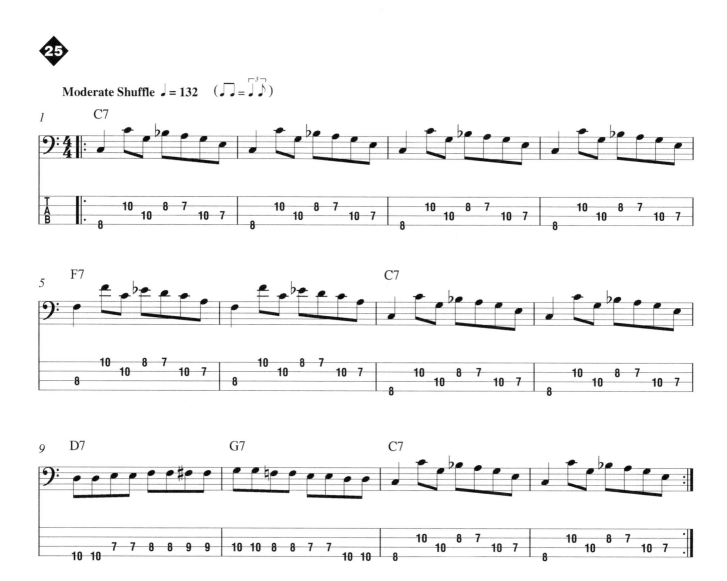

Texas Blues No. 10

Based on the Guitar Slim classic "The Things I Used to Do" (1953), the major triads in this line could be doubled by a guitar or harmonized by a horn section (as on the Slim recording) for a powerful effect. Note the major 7th (C♯, B, and F♯, respectively) "leading tones" on the "and" of beat 4 of measures 8–11, over the I (G), V (D), IV (C), and I chords, which contribute a dollop of extra momentum and create variety.

Performance Tip: As is standard bass practice, use your middle, index, and pinky fingers for the triads in measures 1–7. However, the major 7th in measures 8–11 should be accessed with your index finger.

SWING BLUES

Swing Blues No. 1

Fast swing shuffles are the original source for the hippest walking lines in the blues. As we've seen to varying degrees in earlier figures, a hallmark of the style is smooth, logical connections between changes, which are enhanced by chromatic lines. See the subtleties in measures 1–4, over the I chord (G7), where measures 1–3 include both the ♭7th (F) and the 6th (E) from the Mixolydian mode to define the dominant tonality. Measure 4 ends on the 3rd (B), which also functions as the major 7th "leading tone" of the IV chord (C7) in measure 5. Beginning in measure 6 (IV chord), a long, skillfully crafted line involving chromaticism extends all the way to measure 11 (I chord), the turnaround. Observe the three descending chromatic lines in measures 9–11 (over the V, IV, and I chord, respectively), which provide extraordinary forward motion.

Performance Tip: Play measures 10 and 11 with your ring, middle, and index fingers.

Swing Blues No. 2

Swing blues bass lines tend to rise and fall in register in gentle arcs while also regularly reversing direction—presenting a steady flow of supportive musical ideas. Leaning heavily towards jazz, measures 1–4 below (over the I chord, G7) are bracketed with the root (G) but create plenty of musical tension in between by emphasizing the 2nd (or 9th, A) and by inserting the ♭2nd (A♭) on beat 4 of measure 3 (which functions as a passing note between the 2nd and the root that follows in measure 4). Note the I–VI–II–V changes (G7–E7–A7–D7) in measures 7–10, which substitute for the usual I, I, V, and IV chords. Also, check out how measure 8 (the VI chord) ends on the root (E) after engendering tension with the ♭3rd (G) on beat 1.

Performance Tip: In measure 1, begin with your pinky, followed by your index, middle, and index fingers.

Swing Blues No. 3

Though swing blues bassists often gravitated to the higher registers so as to find their sonic space in large ensembles, the nether regions were not neglected. Check out the muscular propulsion in measures 1–4, over the I chord (G7), and the unusual repetition in measures 5–6 (the IV chord, C7), which produces tension and anticipation. Notice the dynamic and sophisticated lines that connect the I chord to the VI chord (E7) in measures 7–8, where the ♭7th (open D string, measure 8) implies the dominant quality in conjunction with the root (E) that immediately follows. The bass lines for the II–V (A7–D7) chord change in measures 9–10 clearly navigate the change, starting with open-string roots, while connecting directly to the I chord in measure 11.

Performance Tip: Using your index, middle, and ring fingers in measure 10 will lead efficiently to your pinky to play the root (G) on beat 1 of measure 11.

Swing Blues No. 4

The root–3rd–4th–♭5th (G–B–C–C♯/D♭) line in measures 1 and 11, which resolves to the 5th (D) in measures 2 and 12, is a classic walking blues pattern that's so distinct that it could function as a motif while driving the progression forward like a piston. Observe the long run from measure 3 to measure 6, over the I (G7) and IV (C7) chords, which descends for two measures and then ascends for two measures, followed by a dynamic change of phrasing in measures 7–8 (over the I chord). Here, instead of maintaining strict walking quarter notes, the root (G), major 7th (F♯), ♭7th (F), and 6th (E) notes are doubled up to slow the perception of time as a prelude to the ascending two-octave D Mixolydian pattern in measures 9–10, over the V chord (D7). Note how the ascending and descending chromatic pattern in the turnaround (measures 11 and 12) manages to "turn around" the progression without moving to the V chord.

Performance Tip: Unusually, measures 1–4 all start with the pinky.

Swing Blues No. 5

Propulsive triplets in this sophisticated slow blues supply a dollop of forward motion and "swing." As befits a jazz form, the patterns vary greatly, with none repeating exactly, and "sweet" 6th chords are emphasized, as opposed to dominant 7ths or 9ths. This line is what one might find in the jazz-inflected blues of Tiny Grimes, who played with both Screamin' J. Hawkins and Charlie "Yardbird" Parker. Observe how the variety of phrasing allows the progression to "breathe," particularly in measures 4 and 7 (over the I chord, Bb6), which contain straight quarter notes. The turnaround (measures 11 and 12) features an efficient walking pattern that nails each chord change while boosting the momentum via triplets.

Performance Tip: Employ a number of fingerings throughout, utilizing just your index finger for the triplet in measure 8.

RHYTHM & BLUES

R&B No. 1

Similar to the classic R&B of Ray Charles in the fifties, the repetitive patterns in this blues have an element of syncopation in the sixteenth notes, rhythmically reminiscent of the Latin music that was in the air at the time. The II–V (A–D) changes in measures 9 and 10 contain four quarter notes as dynamic contrast to the I (G) and IV (C) chords. Check out the chromatic lines, featuring the 3rd, 4th, ♭5th, and 5th, that follow the root for the I (G) and IV (C) chords in measures 1–8 and 12. Playing the 4th as a quarter note creates anticipation that is rewarded with the rush of sixteenth notes that follow and resolve to the root. Pay attention to the way the line walks from the V chord in measure 10 to the root (G) in measure 11, followed by a dynamic descent to the 3rd (B) on string 3. The I chord pattern from measure 1 is repeated in measure 12 so as to maintain momentum into the next 12-bar blues chorus.

Performance Tip: Play the sixteenth-note runs in measures 1–8 and 11–12 with a ring, pinky, index, and pinky finger combination.

R&B No. 2

The classic Chicago blues octave pattern is turned into a syncopated line, with a suggestive hint of the Afro-Cuban rumba, as was popular in the fifties and sixties. Blues bass and R&B bass often share the same Mixolydian mode lines but the phrasing generally is more syncopated and varied in the latter. At the same time, 12-bar R&B bass progressions tend to be more repetitive, perhaps because, compared to most blues, R&B was "dance music" and the "groove" was of great importance.

Performance Tip: The index and ring fingers are all that are needed throughout this blues.

R&B No. 3

This blues is about as simple and basic a line as possible, with just the root, 3rd, and 5th notes from the major triads of the I, IV, and V chords (which are G, C, and D chords here). However, the Latin syncopation, reminiscent of "Mary Ann" (1956) by Ray Charles, along with the "rumboogie" style of pianist Professor Longhair, transforms the notes into a slinky motif with a sensuous groove. Notice the change to the lower register, from the root (D) to the 3rd (F#), in measure 9 (over the V chord), which breaks up the predictability of the repetitive pattern, while also creating a modicum of dynamic contrast to the I and IV chords. More dynamics, however, are produced in the turnaround (measure 12) via the pumping eighth notes on the root of the V chord (D) for a definitive conclusion to the progression.

Performance Tip: Use your middle, index, and pinky fingers throughout.

R&B No. 4

The more "baroque" version of "R&B No. 3," this pattern incorporates the ♭3rd (C♯/D♭, F♯/G♭, and G♯/A♭, respectively) of the I (B♭), IV (E♭), and V (F) chords from the relative blues scale, where it functions as a "grace note" that leads to the major 3rd. Blues guitarists regularly utilize this technique as a badge of authenticity, though they usually hammer on from the ♭3rd to the major 3rd. A similarly phrased line appears in the rumba-powered "Crosscut Saw" (1967) by Albert King. Check out how the 5th and 6th notes from the Mixolydian mode (absent the ♭7th) produce a "happy," uplifting effect.

Performance Tip: Use the following finger combination throughout: pinky, middle, ring, index, ring, and index.

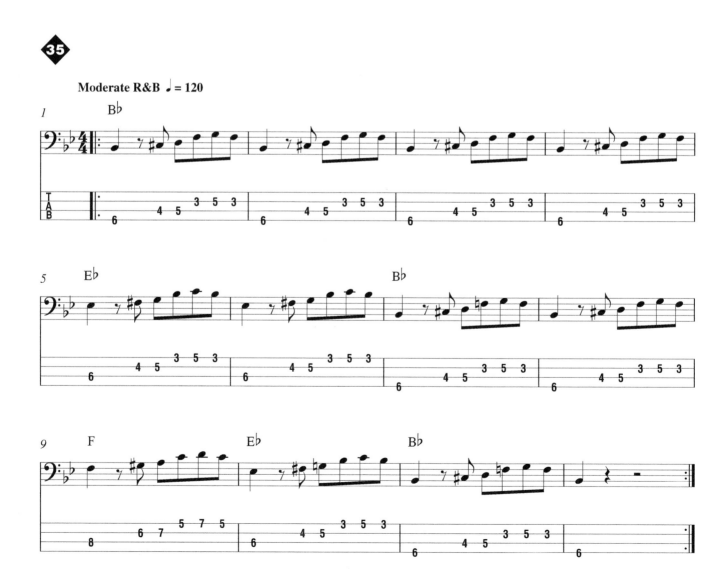

R&B No. 5

The first Motown hit, "Money (That's What I Want)" (1959) by Barrett Strong, incorporates a bass line that is similar to our next example, which functions as a motif and is doubled by piano and/or guitar. The composite blues scale (i.e., blues scale plus Mixolydian mode) not only provides bluesy "grit," but the opportunity to form a chromatic line from the ♭3rd (G and C) to the 4th (A and D) of the I (E) and IV (A) chords, respectively. Since the line for the I and IV chords is a two-measure phrase, it is necessary to make an alteration in measures 9 and 10 for the V (B) and IV chords, which last only one measure here. In this case, the solution to the "musical problem" was solved by creating new lines that produce a "breather" in between the surging I and IV chord patterns. Likewise, the pounding roots (B) in measure 12 offer dynamic contrast.

Performance Tip: Walk up from the ♭3rd to the 4th in measures 1, 3, 5, 7, and 11 with your index, middle, and ring fingers.

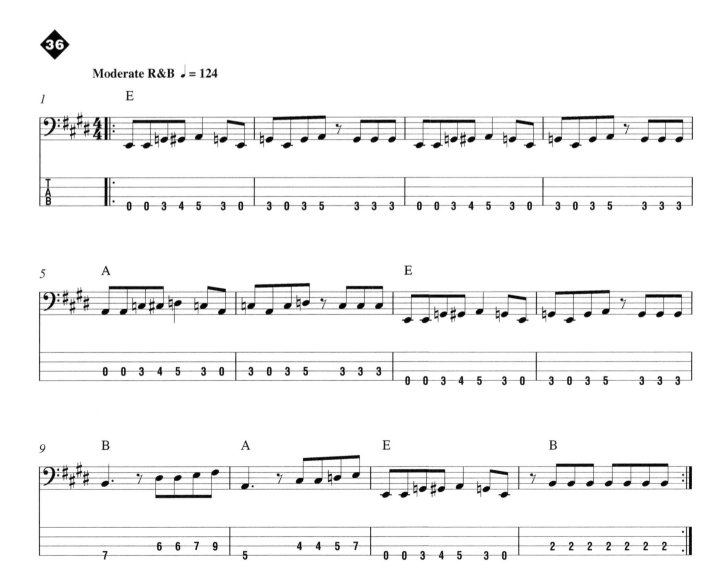

JAZZ BLUES

Jazz Blues No. 1

Jazzy blues bassists are generally freed from having to hew as closely to the prime chord tones as their Chicago and Texas brethren. For example, they may opt to create long lines that do not commence with or even resolve to the root. The result is greater musical tension, providing more anticipation and forward motion. Observe how the I (A7) chord bass line in measures 1–4, below, begins on the 5th (E), touches on the root (A) in measure 3, and walks all the way down to the root of the IV chord (D7) in measure 5 via a chromatic line in measure 4. Also, note how the ascending line in measures 8 and 10, over the I (A7) and V (E7) chords, walks from the root (A and E) to the 2nd (B and F♯), rather than the 3rd (C♯ and G♯), as in more straight-ahead blues bass. A hip nuance occurs on the "and" of beat 4 of measure 10 (V chord), where the second of two eighth notes moves by a half step, from the 3rd (G♯) to the root (A) in measure 11.

Performance Tip: Given the slow blues tempo and quarter notes, your index finger could be employed for most notes, if desired. However, in measure 10, it is recommended to use your middle and index fingers, respectively, for the eighth notes on beat 4.

Jazz Blues No. 2

Minor-key swing tunes are somewhat rare in more traditional blues but not so much in jazz blues. A select number of the notes from the Dorian mode relative to the i (Gm) and iv (Cm) chords neatly conveys the proper harmony, with expected emphasis on the ♭3rd (B♭ and E♭) for each chord. See how the B♭ on beats 3 and 4 of measure 4 (I chord) also functions as the leading tone to the root (C) of the iv chord in measure 5. Similarly, the 2nd (D) on beat 4 of measure 6 leads to the root (G) in measure 7, where a classic descending minor sequence uses "gravity" to advance the momentum. Notice the smooth transition to the ♭VI (E♭) chord in measure 9, which continues on through to the turnaround (measure 12) via a long, flowing line.

Performance Tip: Due to the wide span of intervals in measure 12, including an octave jump, use the following finger combination: index, pinky, pinky, and index.

Jazz Blues No. 3

Shuffling eighth notes "swing" this blues, while passing tones create chromatic lines within the Ionian mode for a fluid, major tonality progression that features the major 7th (A, B, and E) of the I (B♭), II (C), and V (F) chord changes, respectively. The gracefully undulating arc connecting measures 1–8 is especially effective at enhancing the forward motion via numerous half steps, along with the strong 5th–root movement in measures 6–7, over the IV (E♭) and I chords. The descending line that navigates the turnaround (measures 11–12) is unusual. Note the quick half step from beat 4 of the V (F) chord to beat 1 of the first measure, which occurs when you repeat the form.

Performance Tip: Play measure 6 with the following finger combination: middle, middle, index, and pinky.

Jazz Blues No. 4

For the most part, this example avoids the typical blues bass foundation of walking Mixolydian lines that use the root, 3rd, and 5th scale degrees. Instead, root–5th and 5th–root movement creates more dynamics, as seen in measures 5–6, over the IV chord (E♭7); measure 7, over the I chord (B♭7); and measure 8, over the VI chord (G7). Likewise, not all measures start on the root, which creates longer sustained lines and extended forward motion that doesn't resolve until measures 9–12. At this point, the root is needed to outline the crucial II–V–I–V changes. However, a dash of extra forward motion is produced in measure 12 via the 5th (C), 6th (D), ♭7th (D♯/E♭), and root (F) notes.

Performance Tip: Employ your index finger as a small barre to access the root–5th and 5th–root notes in measures 5–7.

Jazz Blues No. 5

Descending Mixolydian lines create the appropriate melancholy ambience for a slow blues, while dynamic ascending triplets and swung eighth notes convey additional momentum. Observe that, melodically, no two measures are the same, while rhythmic variety abounds in measures 1–8. Note the octave jumps in measures 5–6, over the IV (D7/D9) chord—not often found in Chicago or Texas blues—which contribute more dynamics to contrast the fluid run of notes that follow. There are many ways to navigate the I–ii–iii–VI–II–V (A–Bm–C♯m–F♯7–B7–E9) changes in measures 7–10. In measures 7–8, basic root–3rd and root–♭3rd note choices suffice, while the root and a chromatic line in measures 9–10 advance the forward motion to the turnaround. Do not miss the ascending and descending lines in measures 11 and 12, respectively, with the latter "turning around" handsomely to the root in measure 1 (the beginning of the next blues chorus).

Performance Tip: In measure 5, use your middle finger, followed by your pinky, middle, ring, and index fingers; and a similar finger combination in measure 6.

BLUES-ROCK

Blues-Rock No. 1

The classic fifties rock 'n' roll of Little Richard, Fats Domino, and the criminally unsung Larry Williams regularly sported walking Ionian (or the similar Mixolydian) mode lines hopped up for the new "youth music." Again, notice the hint of Latin syncopation, despite the brisk tempo. The drop in register for the V (E) chord adds dynamic contrast similar to "Johnny B. Goode" (1957) by Chuck Berry.

> **Performance Tip:** Use the following finger combination for the I (A) and IV (D) chords: middle, index, pinky, index, and pinky.

Blues-Rock No. 2

In this example, a classic minor pentatonic riff reverses a classic Chicago blues pattern to drive the progression forward with relentless energy. Regularly doubled by guitar, this pattern was a favorite of British blues-rockers and American instrumental groups like the Ventures, and similarly appeared in Little Richard's "Lucille" (1957) and Ray Charles's "What'd I'd Say" (1959). Observe that the root, 5th, ♭7th, and root (octave) riff is a complete, self-contained unit that may be endlessly repeated and recycled. As opposed to "Blues-Rock No. 1," the parallel patterns are so powerful that they withstand the predictability of the progression.

Performance Tip: Use your index and ring fingers for the entire riff.

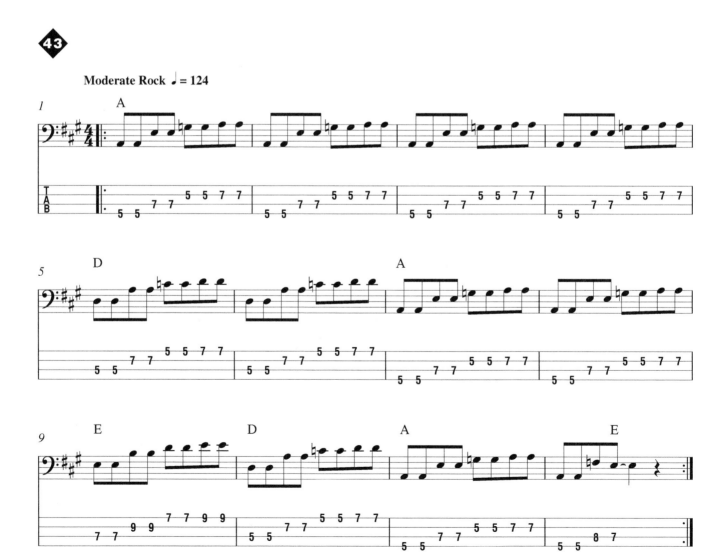

Blues-Rock No. 3

In this example, a rumbling, muscular Mixolydian-mode pattern relative to the I (A) and IV (D) chords provides endless forward motion, due to the addition of the major 7th (G$\sharp$ and C$\sharp$, respectively) on beat 4 of each measure, which leads back to each chord change's root. Measures 9 and 10 employ a similar riff that omits the major 7th for variety. Notice the absence of a turnaround, with the I-chord pattern repeating to maintain forward momentum.

Performance Tip: Begin every measure with your ring finger.

Blues-Rock No. 4

This example takes a step towards rock via a riff and rhythm similar to "Born in Chicago" (1965) by the Paul Butterfield Band. Minor pentatonic scales are often the source material for blues-rock, as exemplified in the I (A), IV (D), and V (E) chord changes. It also is common for the guitarist to play the scales in unison with the bassist. Hence, the progressions tend to be worked out in advance and repeated faithfully throughout the composition. Note how the riff doesn't repeat exactly the same way over the course of the three changes (which is a common pitfall with simple pentatonic riff progressions). For example, check out measure 6 (IV chord), where the E and G notes (beat 4) from the I chord appear, rather than the same A and C notes found in measure 5. Additionally, see measure 9 (V chord), where the major 7th (D#/Eb) functions as a passing tone between the root (E) and the root (D) of the IV chord in measure 10.

Performance Tip: Utilize a ring-ring-index finger combination for the riffs in measures 1–5, 7–8, and 11.

Blues-Rock No. 5

Both "Green Onions" (1962) by Booker T & the MGs and "Help Me" (1963) by Sonny Boy Williamson II lay claim to this signature bass line, which apparently was concocted by original MGs bassist Lewis Steinberg. Though it utilizes the exact same relative minor pentatonic scale patterns for the I (E), IV (A), and V (B) chords, the line is so distinct and powerfully propulsive that it bears repeating. Like many other blues-rock bass lines, this figure often is doubled by guitar for an even bigger kick in the pants.

Performance Tip: As opposed to most blues-based lines, the right-hand thumb can be used throughout.

FUNK BLUES

Funk Blues No. 1

The following example employs a classic first-generation funk line similar to "Twine Time" (1964) by Alvin Cash & the Crawlers and the immortal "Shotgun" by Junior Walker & the All Stars (1965). Funk blues often are built upon minor pentatonic scales, instead of the Mixolydian or Ionian modes. Observe how starting the line on the root (D and G) and ending on the 5th (A and D) for the I (D7) and IV (G9) chords, respectively, creates an automatic cycle of 4ths, which may be repeated indefinitely. However, note that, in measures 6 and 10 (IV chord), the A and C notes from the I chord—functioning as the 2nd and 4th, respectively—are substituted to encourage resolution back to the D chord. In addition, the V (A9) chord change in measure 9 incorporates the D and F notes—functioning as the 4th and ♭6th, respectively—from the IV chord. These notes make for a smoother transition to the IV chord in measure 10.

Performance Tip: The ring and index fingers may be used throughout.

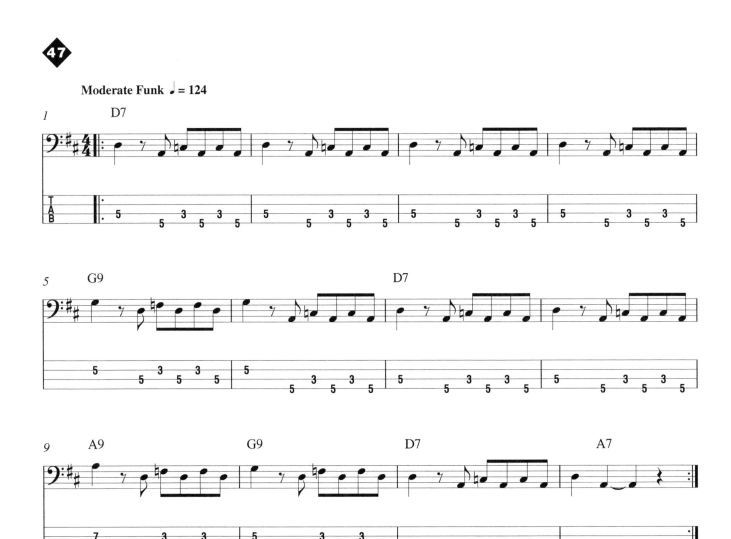

Funk Blues No. 2

Octaves are one of the cornerstones of funk, as prominently heard on Sly & the Family Stone's "Thank You Falettinme Be Mice Elf Again" (1970) with the great bassist Larry Graham "snapping and slapping." In the following example, check out the ascending chromatic line on beats 3–4 of each measure, which walks back up to the root (G and C) of the I (G7) and IV (C9) chords, respectively, in dynamic contrast to the syncopated octave riff that is derived from the minor pentatonic scale. To avoid needless repetition, measures 9 and 10 (the V to IV change) omit the octave jump and, instead, alternate the root with the ♭7th (C and B♭, respectively) for some blues-approved dominant tonality.

> **Performance Tip:** Jump the octave with your index and ring fingers in measures 1–8 and 11–12, making a swift change from your middle finger on the final eighth note of each preceding measure.

Funk Blues No. 3

The Mixolydian mode provides a more upbeat, melodic scale from which to concoct this variation of the octave jump, reminiscent of James Brown's "Cold Sweat" (1967). As in "Funk Blues No. 2," the I (A7) and IV (D9) chords utilize octaves, while the V (E9), IV, and I changes in measures 9–11 turn traditional walking blues bass lines into funky riffs via syncopation. Note how measures 9–12 flow smoothly, despite the syncopation, thanks to chromatic lines and the 3rd (C♯) at the end of measure 11, which resolves nicely to the root (A) at the beginning of measure 12. Resolution from the 3rd to the root also occurs in measures 1–8, over the I and IV chords.

Performance Tip: In measures 1–8, use your index, middle, and pinky fingers on frets 4, 5, and 7, respectively.

Funk Blues No. 4

Seventies funk band Parliament/Funkadelic and former JB bassist Bootsy Collins influenced younger blues bass players such as Aron Burton and Johnny "B. Goode" Gayden, who backed Albert "The Iceman" Collins. This example shows one take on how they might approach blues. With their sixteenth notes and strategically placed eighth-note rests, the minor pentatonic patterns for the I (D7) and IV (G9) chords in measures 1–8 and 11 of this example emit some serious "stink." As opposed to the other musical figures, these patterns are arranged in two-measure phrases that feature a hefty three-beat rest in every other measure for dramatic dynamics. The lines contain the root, 5th, and ♭7th notes, with emphasis on the ♭7th to complement the chord changes. Observe how the 5th (A and D) on the "and" of beat 4 of measures 1, 3, 5, 7, and 11 (I and IV chords) logically resolves to the root in measures 2, 4, 6, 8, and 12. Octaves in measures 9 and 10, over the V (A9) and IV chords, respectively, break the repetition and boost forward motion towards the turnaround via additional eighth notes.

Performance Tip: Alternation between your right-hand's index and middle fingers is absolutely required for efficiency and funky staccato phrasing.

Funk Blues No. 5

This funky blues *pops* with sixteenth-note roots (A and D) punctuating each two-measure riff, pushing the envelope of funk blues into maximum odiferous territory in measures 1–8, over the I (A7) and IV (D9) chords. Check out how the ascending chromatic lines on beats 3–4 of measures 1, 3, 5, 7, and 11 end on the bluesy ♭5th (D♯/E♭ and G♯/A♭) for a dash of musical tension (as opposed to resolving smoothly back to the root, for instance). However, in order to avoid an awkward transition between chords in measures 1–8, the measures preceding the chord changes have a dynamic rest on beats 3–4. Stuttered walking lines in measures 9 and 10 break the flow between beats 2 and 3 to maintain continuity with the rhythms in measures 1–8.

> **Performance Tip:** Play the root notes in measures 1–8 and 11–12 with your ring finger. The eighth-note rest on beat 3 will allow time to get to the 3rd (C♯ and F♯) that follows via the index finger.

Moderate Funk ♩ = 120